**COMPOSER SHOWCASE**
HAL LEONARD STUDENT PIANO LIBRARY

# Les Petites Images

## ORIGINAL PIANO SOLOS IN IMPRESSIONIST STYLE

### BY JENNIFER LINN

## CONTENTS

Editor: Margaret Otwell

Cover Painting: "Seine at Asnières" by Pierre-Auguste Renoir, 1879

ISBN 978-1-4234-1139-0

**HAL • LEONARD® CORPORATION**
7777 W. BLUEMOUND RD. P.O. BOX 13819 MILWAUKEE, WI 53213

In Australia Contact:
**Hal Leonard Australia Pty. Ltd.**
4 Lentara Court
Cheltenham, Victoria, 3192 Australia
Email: ausadmin@halleonard.com

Visit Hal Leonard Online at
**www.halleonard.com**

# Performance Notes

## Tonnerre sur les plaines (Thunder On The Plains)

Imagination can be the magic ingredient that draws students to the music, and the dramatic story line that unfolds in "Thunder On The Plains" will certainly spark their creative minds and encourage an expressive performance. A lonely shepherd breaks the silence with the opening "flute solo," and is joined by an echoing voice in the left hand and a third voice joining in harmony, creating a cheerful pastoral scene. Suddenly, thunder (the cross-hand fifths in m. 9-12) booms across the valley! Just as the thunder subsides and the shepherds "sigh" in relief (m. 19), a sudden rain shower erupts (m. 20). As the storm is whisked away as quickly as it came (by the *glissando* in m. 27), the lingering resonant strings convey the image of a shimmering rainbow. The shepherd's flute returns to the opening scene and the final melody signals a peaceful ending to the day.

## L'oiseau-mouche (Hummingbird)

On a family trip to Colorado, we hung a hummingbird feeder outside on the porch, and the buzzing and whistling sounds of the literally dozens of hummingbirds fighting for a spot at the feeder was the inspiration for this piece. I wanted to create a piece for my young students that would introduce them to new ways of playing the piano outside of the familiar 5-finger hand positions found in their method books. I wanted them to be able to create new sounds on the piano using interlocking technique, interesting harmonic colors and repeating patterns. The goal was to compose a piece with an impressionist sound that even the very young pianist could play. The result is a piece that indeed sounds much more difficult than it is actually to perform.

Introduce the piece by first showing students how the R.H. pattern of only two notes (C, E) repeats for thirteen measures. Then help them find the two "sets" of black-key patterns (D♯, F♯ and F♯, A♯) using fingers 4 and 2. The descending fifth in m. 3 should be familiar for them to read. Be sure to demonstrate how the hands can work comfortably together even in crowded situations. The introduction of 6/8 meter may be a new challenge to some students, but the constantly moving eighth notes make it naturally easy to count. Students will enjoy the new physical challenge and the surprisingly sophisticated sounds they can now play.

## Astéroïdes (Asteroids)

Dynamics play a key role in creating this musical image. The carefully placed *crescendos* and *diminuendos* give a dimension to the sound that suggests celestial objects coming dangerously close and then drifting harmlessly away! The use of the whole-tone scale provides a wonderful opportunity to encourage students to improvise or compose their own piece using this pattern. Exploring the mysterious-sounding intervals (minor 9ths and tri-tones) will give students some new colors in their musical crayon box. Crossovers and a broad keyboard range also give students a chance to move freely and experience new technical skills at the piano. In m. 37 the R.H. can play the *glissando* with the thumb nail on the white keys while the L.H. is stationed one octave lower on the two black keys. It is almost as if the R.H. white-key *glissando* is chasing the L.H., which hops down the keyboard on the two black keys! In m. 39 let the crazy roar continue to ring by holding the damper pedal down. While still holding down the pedal, play the last chord silently by using a slow keystroke, and *then* finally release the pedal suddenly. The eerie sound that is left is just the "ashes" of vibrating strings.

## Le grand "dièse" blanc (The Great White "Sharp")

The hunt is on for the single elusive "white sharp" hidden somewhere in this piece. As this humorous march begins, the music searches "high and low," but the only sharps to be found are on the black keys. The special "white sharp" surprise suddenly appears after a dramatic half rest, complete with *fermata* "eyes" and "sharp teeth" accents in m. 28! Students will strengthen their technique with strong *staccato* triads in both the R.H. and L.H. and will gain skill and confidence playing on the black keys. Hand crossings are numerous, but easy to master because of the repeating patterns. The student who may be locked into playing only in certain "positions" will experience choreography at the keyboard that sounds difficult but is fun and easy to play once the patterns become familiar.

## Le frelon furieux (The Mad Hornet)

Inspired by a rather traumatic childhood memory, "The Mad Hornet" includes the musical expression mark *dangereux* for good reason. One summer afternoon, while I was riding in the back seat of the car, an uninvited guest flew in through the open car window. It sounded like an entire hive, but as the solo scoundrel buzzed around my head I naturally started to panic. My mother assured me that "they won't bother *you* if you don't bother *them*." With flailing arms and desperate screeches I bullied the poor hornet into such a furious state that it had no choice but to sting me precisely on my eyelid. My eye swelled shut and over the next few days turned several shades of purple! Thankfully, the injury appeared more "dangerous" than in its actual "bite." Students playing this piece will surely have a "buzzing tale of terror" of their own to tell! Careful coordination between the hands and faithful observance of all *staccato* and accent markings will assure the performer and listener of a daring musical adventure!

## Le fin d'hiver (Winter's End)

In this solo, the direction *commencez lentement* (begin slowly) evokes the image of a frozen brook gradually coming to life. The hands need to work together to create a seamless motion, and students will need to match the tone quality of both thumbs to avoid interrupting the musical flow. Careful voicing on the *tenuto* notes will bring out the spinning melody, and strict observance of tempo variances (*peu a peu animant* in m. 7 and *ralentir* in m. 21) will enhance the musical image of a stream warmed by springtime's arrival, but still delayed by Winter's frosty chill.

## Voilers dans le vent (Sailboats In The Wind)

Balance and voicing are critical skills for intermediate students to master. With that in mind, this piece purposefully begins with the melody in the L.H. Ask the student to finger the R.H. patterns silently in his lap as he plays the L.H. melody on the piano with beautiful tone. Next, he can finger the R.H. silently on the keys while still playing the L.H. When the student can do this successfully, he may add more weight gradually to the R.H. until he achieves the desired balance. The 6/8 meter was a natural choice for these fast-moving sailboats and reinforces the meter originally introduced in "Hummingbird." This final solo in the collection offers two additional challenges to the student as well: the rolled chords in mm. 76-77, and the introduction of the triplet versus duplet polyrhythm in m. 78. This single measure of polyrhythm is an obtainable task and will prepare students for similar rhythmic patterns found in two of my other collections: *Les Petites Impressions* and *American Impressions*. My deepest wish is to prepare students well for the ultimate goal of playing the great masterworks of Debussy and Ravel.

---

*This collection is dedicated to Dr. Reid Alexander, a true friend who has inspired me through his steadfast passion for teaching, his natural compassion and desire to help all students, and his sincere devotion and extensive contribution to the field of piano pedagogy.*

# Glossary Of French Terms

| FRENCH | TRANSLATION | FRENCH | TRANSLATION |
|---|---|---|---|
| *amusant* | amusing | *laisser vibrer* | let ring |
| *animant* | getting faster (accelerando) | *lent* | slow |
| *animez* | lively | *lointain* | distant |
| *au mouvement* | resume original tempo (a tempo) | *marqué* | marked, accented |
| | | *menaçant* | threatening |
| *augmentez* | increase | *modéré* | moderate |
| *bourdonnant* | humming | *mystérieux* | mysterious |
| *calme* | calm | *petite* | little |
| *cédez* | slow down (ritenuto) | *peu à peu* | gradually |
| *chanté* | singing | *la pluie soudaine* | a sudden rainshower |
| *comme une flûte de Pan* | like a shepherd's flute | *plus* | more |
| *commencez lentement* | begin slowly | *plus près* | coming closer |
| *coulant* | flowing | *précisément* | precisely |
| *doucement* | softly, gently | *première (1re) mouvement* | Tempo I |
| *doux* | tender, sweet | *presser* | compress the tempo (stringendo) |
| *égale et dangereux* | even and dangerous | *ralentir* | to slow down (ritardando) |
| *explosif* | explosive | *rapide* | quick |
| *expressif* | expressive | *retenant, retenu* | holding back, held back (ritenuto) |
| *facile* | easy | | |
| *hésitant* | hesitating | *très* | very |
| *images* | pictures, images | *un peu* | a little |
| *jusqu'á la fin* | to the end | | |

# Tonnerre sur les plaines
## Thunder On The Plains

Jennifer Linn

*Chanté, comme une flûte de Pan* (♩ = 84)

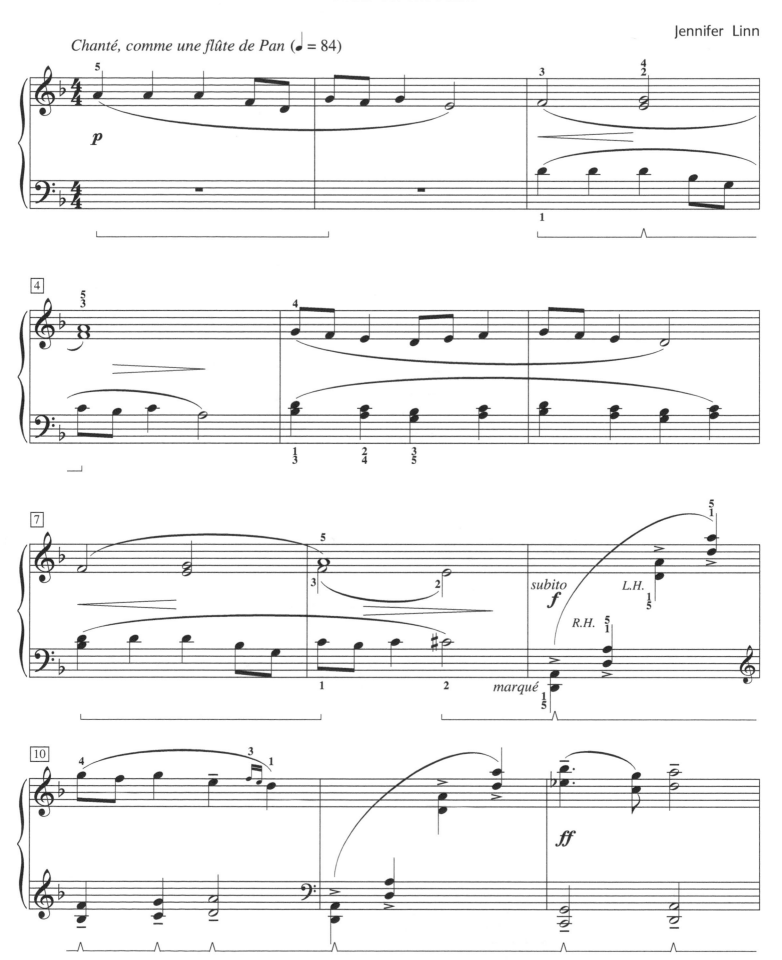

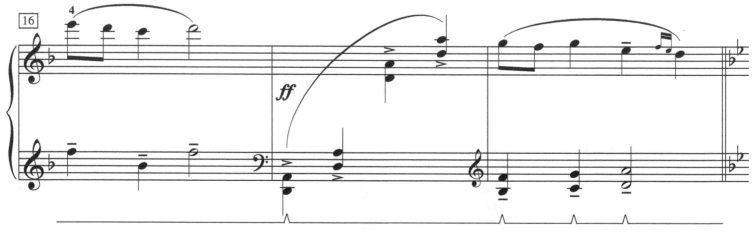

un peu retenu - - - - - - - - - - - - - - - -//*animez et augmentez*

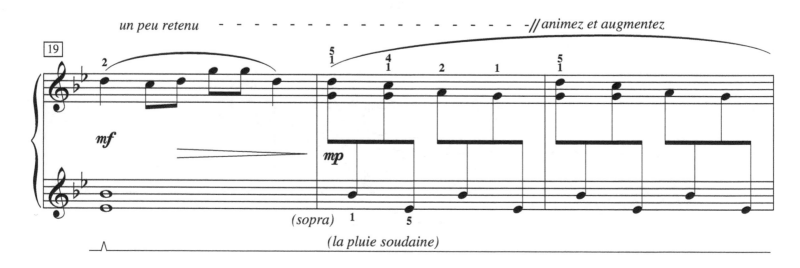

(sopra)

(la pluie soudaine)

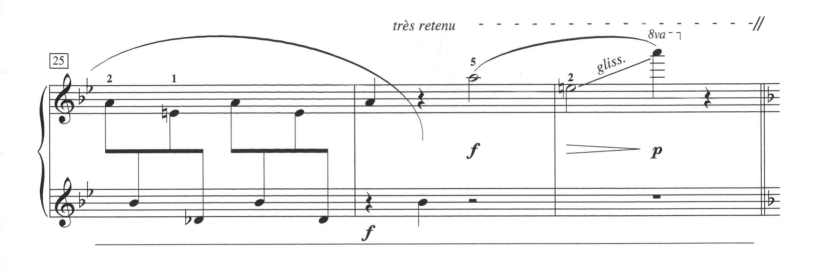

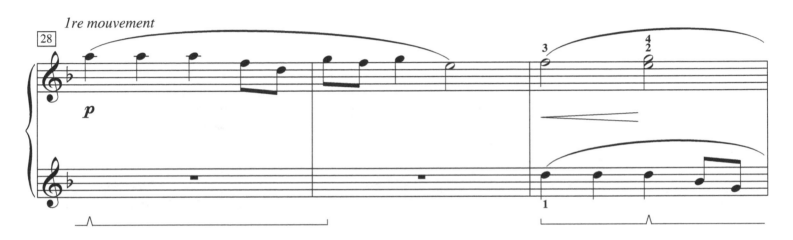

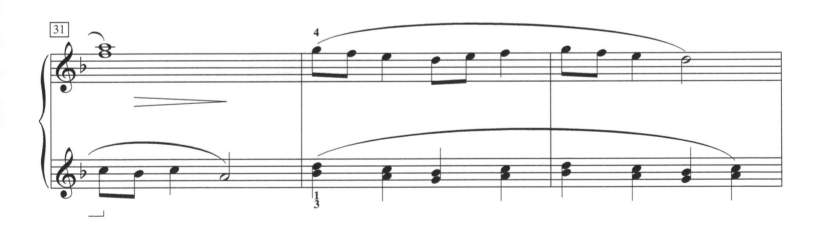

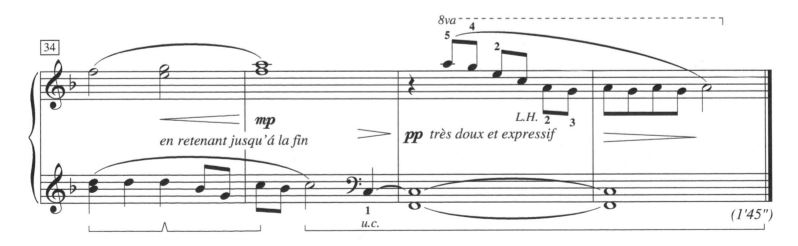

# L'oiseau-mouche

## Hummingbird

Jennifer Linn

(31″)

# Astéroïdes
## Asteroids

Jennifer Linn

# Le grand "dièse" blanc

### The Great White "Sharp"

Jennifer Linn

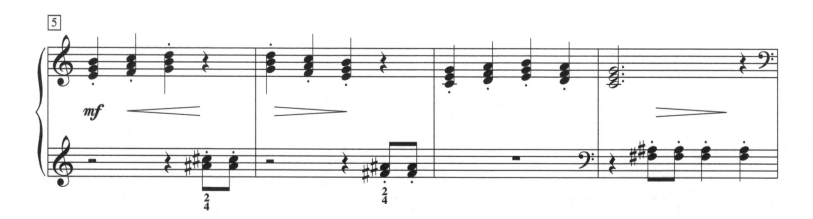

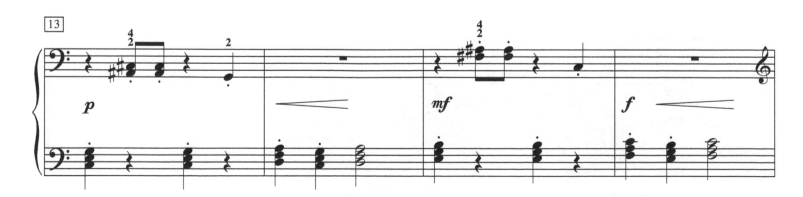

# Le frelon furieux

## The Mad Hornet

Jennifer Linn

En animant peu à peu

1er mouvement

# Le fin d'hiver

## Winter's End

Jennifer Linn

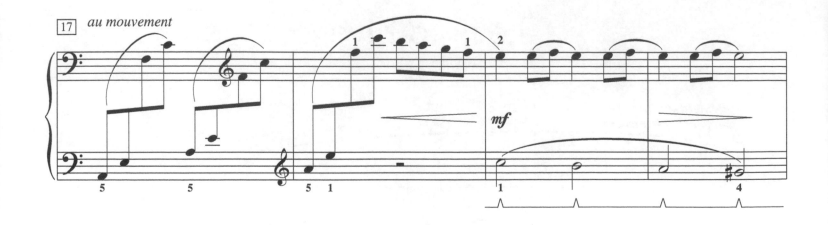

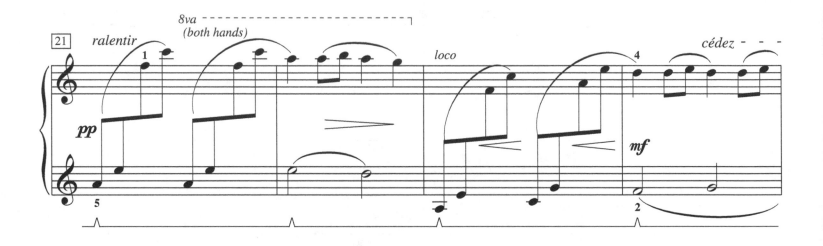

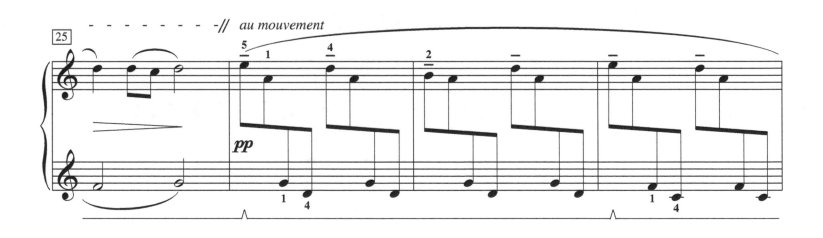

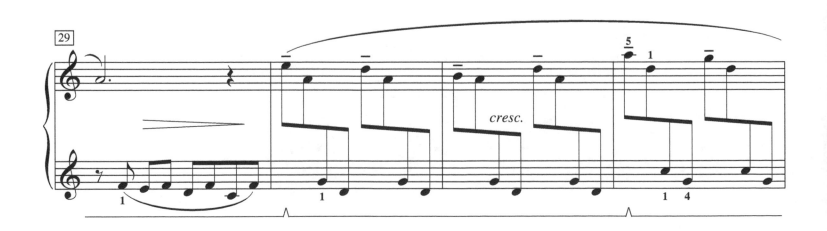

(1'16")

# Voiliers dans le vent

## Sailboats In The Wind

Jennifer Linn

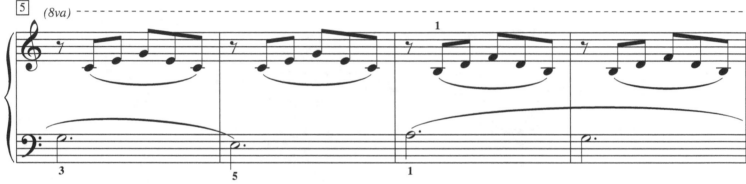

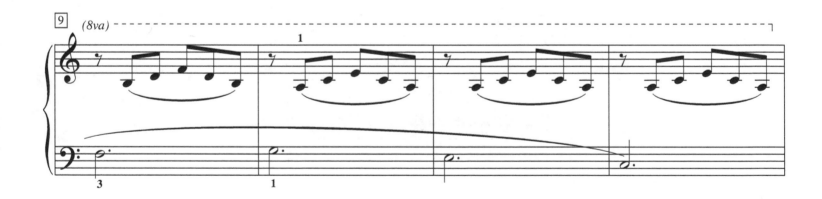

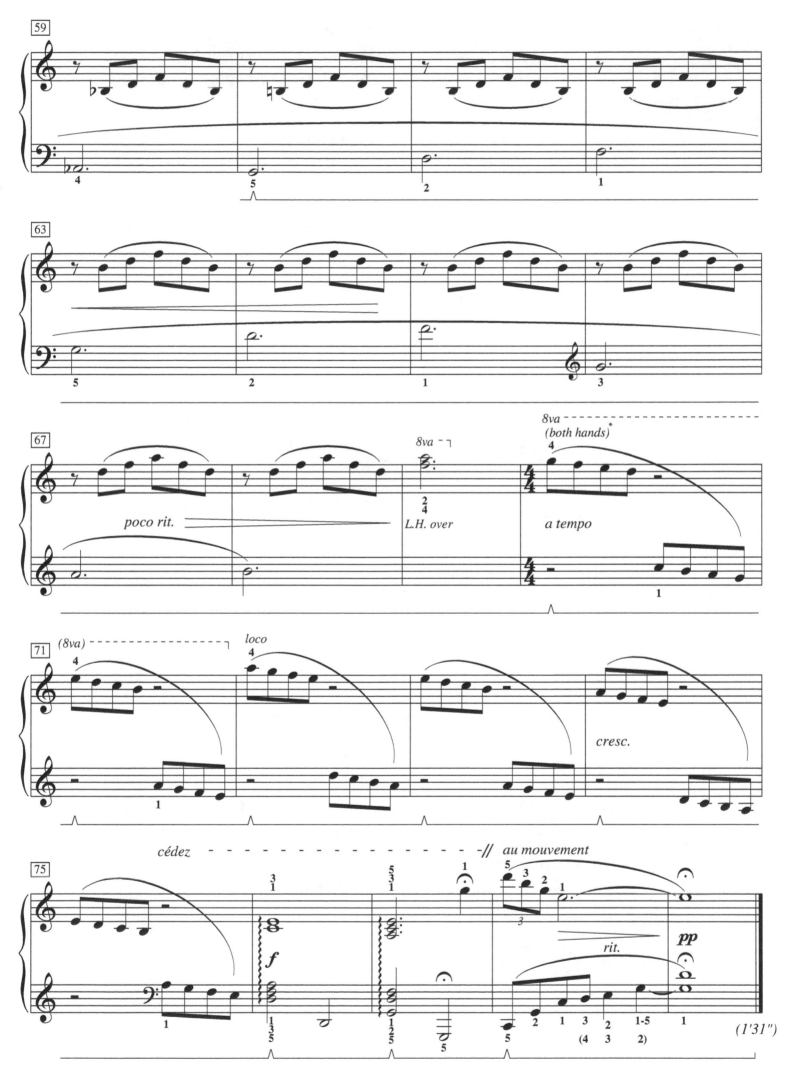

This series showcases great original piano music from our **Hal Leonard Student Piano Library** family of composers. Carefully graded for easy selection.

## BILL BOYD

**JAZZ BITS (AND PIECES)**
*Early Intermediate Level*
00290312 11 Solos......................$7.99

**JAZZ DELIGHTS**
*Intermediate Level*
00240435 11 Solos......................$8.99

**JAZZ FEST**
*Intermediate Level*
00240436 10 Solos......................$8.99

**JAZZ PRELIMS**
*Early Elementary Level*
00290032 12 Solos......................$7.99

**JAZZ SKETCHES**
*Intermediate Level*
00220001 8 Solos........................$8.99

**JAZZ STARTERS**
*Elementary Level*
00290425 10 Solos......................$8.99

**JAZZ STARTERS II**
*Late Elementary Level*
00290434 11 Solos......................$7.99

**JAZZ STARTERS III**
*Late Elementary Level*
00290465 12 Solos......................$8.99

**THINK JAZZ!**
*Early Intermediate Level*
00290417 Method Book...........$12.99

### TONY CARAMIA

**JAZZ MOODS**
*Intermediate Level*
00296728 8 Solos........................$6.95

**SUITE DREAMS**
*Intermediate Level*
00296775 4 Solos........................$6.99

### SONDRA CLARK

**DAKOTA DAYS**
*Intermediate Level*
00296521 5 Solos........................$6.95

**FLORIDA FANTASY SUITE**
*Intermediate Level*
00296766 3 Duets.......................$7.95

**THREE ODD METERS**
*Intermediate Level*
00296472 3 Duets.......................$6.95

### MATTHEW EDWARDS

**CONCERTO FOR
YOUNG PIANISTS**
FOR 2 PIANOS, FOUR HANDS
*Intermediate Level Book/CD*
00296356 3 Movements ..........$19.99

**CONCERTO NO. 2 IN G MAJOR**
FOR 2 PIANOS, 4 HANDS
*Intermediate Level Book/CD*
00296670 3 Movements............$17.99

## PHILLIP KEVEREN

**MOUSE ON A MIRROR**
*Late Elementary Level*
00296361 5 Solos........................$8.99

**MUSICAL MOODS**
*Elementary/Late Elementary Level*
00296714 7 Solos........................$6.99

**SHIFTY-EYED BLUES**
*Late Elementary Level*
00296374 5 Solos........................$7.99

### CAROL KLOSE

**THE BEST OF CAROL KLOSE**
*Early to Late Intermediate Level*
00146151 15 Solos....................$12.99

**CORAL REEF SUITE**
*Late Elementary Level*
00296354 7 Solos........................$7.50

**DESERT SUITE**
*Intermediate Level*
00296667 6 Solos........................$7.99

**FANCIFUL WALTZES**
*Early Intermediate Level*
00296473 5 Solos........................$7.95

**GARDEN TREASURES**
*Late Intermediate Level*
00296787 5 Solos........................$8.50

**ROMANTIC EXPRESSIONS**
*Intermediate to Late Intermediate Level*
00296923 5 Solos........................$8.99

**WATERCOLOR MINIATURES**
*Early Intermediate Level*
00296848 7 Solos........................$7.99

### JENNIFER LINN

**AMERICAN IMPRESSIONS**
*Intermediate Level*
00296471 6 Solos........................$8.99

**ANIMALS HAVE FEELINGS TOO**
*Early Elementary/Elementary Level*
00147789 8 Solos........................$8.99

**AU CHOCOLAT**
*Late Elementary/Early Intermediate Level*
00298110 7 Solos........................$8.99

**CHRISTMAS IMPRESSIONS**
*Intermediate Level*
00296706 8 Solos........................$8.99

**JUST PINK**
*Elementary Level*
00296722 9 Solos........................$8.99

**LES PETITES IMAGES**
*Late Elementary Level*
00296664 7 Solos........................$8.99

**LES PETITES IMPRESSIONS**
*Intermediate Level*
00296355 6 Solos........................$8.99

**REFLECTIONS**
*Late Intermediate Level*
00296843 5 Solos........................$8.99

**TALES OF MYSTERY**
*Intermediate Level*
00296769 6 Solos........................$8.99

## LYNDA LYBECK-ROBINSON

**ALASKA SKETCHES**
*Early Intermediate Level*
00119637 8 Solos........................$8.99

**AN AWESOME ADVENTURE**
*Late Elementary Level*
00137563 8 Solos........................$7.99

**FOR THE BIRDS**
*Early Intermediate/Intermediate Level*
00237078 9 Solos........................$8.99

**WHISPERING WOODS**
*Late Elementary Level*
00275905 9 Solos........................$8.99

### MONA REJINO

**CIRCUS SUITE**
*Late Elementary Level*
00296665 5 Solos........................$8.99

**COLOR WHEEL**
*Early Intermediate Level*
00201951 6 Solos........................$9.99

**IMPRESIONES DE ESPAÑA**
*Intermediate Level*
00337520 6 Solos........................$8.99

**IMPRESSIONS OF NEW YORK**
*Intermediate Level*
00364212....................................$8.99

**JUST FOR KIDS**
*Elementary Level*
00296840 8 Solos........................$7.99

**MERRY CHRISTMAS MEDLEYS**
*Intermediate Level*
00296799 5 Solos........................$8.99

**MINIATURES IN STYLE**
*Intermediate Level*
00148088 6 Solos........................$8.99

**PORTRAITS IN STYLE**
*Early Intermediate Level*
00296507 6 Solos........................$8.99

### EUGÉNIE ROCHEROLLE

**CELEBRATION SUITE**
*Intermediate Level*
00152724 3 Duets.......................$8.99

**ENCANTOS ESPAÑOLES
(SPANISH DELIGHTS)**
*Intermediate Level*
00125451 6 Solos........................$8.99

**JAMBALAYA**
*Intermediate Level*
00296654 2 Pianos, 8 Hands.....$12.99
00296725 2 Pianos, 4 Hands.......$7.95

**JEROME KERN CLASSICS**
*Intermediate Level*
00296577 10 Solos....................$12.99

**LITTLE BLUES CONCERTO**
*Early Intermediate Level*
00142801 2 Pianos, 4 Hands......$12.99

**TOUR FOR TWO**
*Late Elementary Level*
00296832 6 Duets.......................$9.99

**TREASURES**
*Late Elementary/Early Intermediate Level*
00296924 7 Solos........................$8.99

## JEREMY SISKIND

**BIG APPLE JAZZ**
*Intermediate Level*
00278209 8 Solos........................$8.99

**MYTHS AND MONSTERS**
*Late Elementary/Early Intermediate Level*
00148148 9 Solos........................$8.99

### CHRISTOS TSITSAROS

**DANCES FROM AROUND
THE WORLD**
*Early Intermediate Level*
00296688 7 Solos........................$8.99

**FIVE SUMMER PIECES**
*Late Intermediate/Advanced Level*
00361235 5 Solos......................$12.99

**LYRIC BALLADS**
*Intermediate/Late Intermediate Level*
00102404 6 Solos........................$8.99

**POETIC MOMENTS**
*Intermediate Level*
00296403 8 Solos........................$8.99

**SEA DIARY**
*Early Intermediate Level*
00253486 9 Solos........................$8.99

**SONATINA HUMORESQUE**
*Late Intermediate Level*
00296772 3 Movements.............$6.99

**SONGS WITHOUT WORDS**
*Intermediate Level*
00296506 9 Solos........................$9.99

**THREE PRELUDES**
*Early Advanced Level*
00130747 3 Solos........................$8.99

**THROUGHOUT THE YEAR**
*Late Elementary Level*
00296723 12 Duets.....................$6.95

### ADDITIONAL COLLECTIONS

**AT THE LAKE**
*by Elvina Pearce*
*Elementary/Late Elementary Level*
00131642 10 Solos and Duets.....$7.99

**CHRISTMAS FOR TWO**
*by Dan Fox*
*Early Intermediate Level*
00290069 13 Duets....................$8.99

**CHRISTMAS JAZZ**
*by Mike Springer*
*Intermediate Level*
00296525 6 Solos........................$8.99

**COUNTY RAGTIME FESTIVAL**
*by Fred Kern*
*Intermediate Level*
00296882 7 Solos........................$7.99

**LITTLE JAZZERS**
*by Jennifer Watts*
*Elementary/Late Elementary Level*
00154573 9 Solos........................$8.99

**PLAY THE BLUES!**
*by Luann Carman*
*Early Intermediate Level*
00296357 10 Solos......................$9.99

**ROLLER COASTERS & RIDES**
*by Jennifer & Mike Watts*
*Intermediate Level*
00131144 8 Duets.......................$8.99

Prices, contents, and availability subject to change without notice.